GREAT CITIES OF THE WORLD — OLD HONG KONG

Li Hung Chang, director of the Board of Foreign Affairs in China, photographed with the Governor of Hong Kong Sir Henry Blake at Government House in 1900.

GREAT CITIES OF THE WORLD

OLD HONG KONG

FormAsia

Published by
FormAsia
2301 Sunning Plaza
10 Hysan Avenue
Hong Kong

Written by Trea Wiltshire
Designed by Robert Hookham/Format Limited
Compiled by Frank Fischbeck
Edited by Zenobia Barlow Wetzell
Typeset by TM Typesetting Limited
Printed by Paramount Printing Company Limited
First Edition: Hong Kong, November 1987
Second Edition, Hong Kong, July 1988
Third Edition (Revised): Hong Kong, September 1989
ISBN No. 962-7283-01-0

An Enduring Document of Hong Kong's History

Frank Fischbeck

For a guarded moment, China opened its doors to the ever curious foreigner and his ubiquitous camera. It was 1971, and a gaggle of foreign reporters and photographers accompanied thirteen ping pong players to an impressive display of courtesy and hospitality at matches played in Peking, Shanghai and Canton. The Chinese hosts smiled gently though reluctantly for the cameras in a campaign coined "Ping Pong Diplomacy" by the world press.

The "great wall" had come down, and through ever widening cracks, the lens could focus on the once forbidden sight of the last great hidden empire. In an urge to modernize the camera — long considered a hostile instrument of evil — now served the Party in an effort to demystify China; still the shutter would catch glimpses of an ancient culture shrouded in the mythical past.

And yet it was not always so. In the pioneering days of Hong Kong, as the Opium Wars raged to a close and the last curls of smoke twisted into the blue haze of illicit divans, photographers persevered under wretched conditions contending with shortages of requisite photographic equipment and supplies, heat and debilitating fevers, and the lethal hostility of the Chinese.

In 1851, the first recorded photograph of China — a nine-inch square salted print from a calotype negative of a five-story pagoda in Canton — is credited to a British surgeon Dr. John McCosh. Then, in 1860, two prominent photographers, Michel Rossier and Felix Beato, who arrived in Hong Kong with the Anglo-French Expeditionary Force, were to record with great diligence, the strife, conflict and turmoil of the Chinese coast.

With the creation of "The Firm" — by two peripatetic fellows named Howard and Weed — an archive began to be compiled of the work of adventurous photographers who arrived in the colony, set up shop, then departed in a state of commercial collapse and bankruptcy. A decade later, under the guidance of Matthew Miller whose forte was studio portraiture almost modern in approach, the holdings of "The Firm" had swelled to an impressive collection of glass plates and negatives encompassing the work of eleven failed photographic establishments.

Another important contributor to the

photographic documentation of the history of Hong Kong was John Thomson who, with profound sympathy and insatiable curiosity for the Chinese people, stayed from 1868 to 1872.

The last of this distinguished group of early photographers was D K Griffith who spent twenty years in the South and recounted the dangers and difficulties he experienced in practicing his "art-science" in China. "This hostility by the Natives," wrote Griffith, "lies in the strange belief that the photographic image is the soul of the original, the withdrawal of which produces death a month or a year later". Chinese photographers, who numbered fourteen by 1872, experienced even worse fate and operated only in the relatively enlightened cities in the South. Griffith was acutely aware of the problems encountered by Chinese photographers. "The native artist has little support from his countrymen," he said, "In my own case I have had my chair torn to pieces on the road, my coolies beaten, and my camera broken.. in the case of a Chinaman, he would have fared much worse".

Neither the mandarin with his morbid fear of the photographic process, nor the transient foreigner, who left the colony for "home" clutching his photo-album as a source of memories in the autumn of his life, were to provide Hong Kong with any enduring document of its history. When "The Firm" came to an end in 1877, with the disposition of its archive unknown, Hong Kong was to lose the only comprehensive collection of its recorded past.

Old Hong Kong is the result of the efforts of yet another foreign photographer who too came for a brief adventure and stayed to resurrect the ideals of "The Firm" by patiently collecting faded photographs from forgotten albums in musty libraries now scattered far and wide. However the winds of change blow on Hong Kong, this book documents the transformation, by two great empires, of a trading post on the South China Coast to one of the great cities of the world.

Hong Kong — Striding with the Bold Effrontery of Empire

Trea Wiltshire

When the curious eye of the camera first focused on China in the 1850s, it recorded an incredible series of double images: the slow death of the last dynasty to rule China; and the triumphant rise of a new empire spawned by a tiny island on the other side of the world.

The camera captured a myriad of images: jostling street scenes and dim punkah-cooled interiors; wax moustachios and swinging pigtails; starched collars and embroidered silk; palaces, pagodas and palanquins...

But a single symbolic image also emerged.

The Imperial Dragon, emblem of emperors, symbol of strength and vigilance, was weak and deluded. Steeped in images of its own ancient splendour, it was unable to respond to the challenge of a new era.

And around the Middle Kingdom paced Britain's Imperial Lion, eager to plant its paw on the proud empire which had forbidden it a foothold.

Riding high on a tide of exploration, trade and technology, the British Empire was approaching its apogee.

The nation's industrial strength and naval superiority — plus an unflinching conviction that it was born to rule — assured it an empire that would eventually cover a quarter of the earth.

Little wonder the Dragon eyed the Lion with dark suspicion. For the pattern of empire-building was already established. First came missionaries and merchants; then followed conquest and the flag.

China had never in its long history treated other nations as equals, nor traded with them to any great extent. Its ignorance of the world beyond the Middle Kingdom was profound; its conviction of its own superiority was complete.

Vassal states on the outer limits of its empire were tolerated and allowed to bring tributes to the Emperor, the Son of Heaven.

"When they come to the Celestial Empire to bring tributes," wrote a court official, "all their envoys perform the ceremony of the three kneelings and the nine knockings of the head."

When British ambassadors — who in turn considered themselves vastly superior — refused to perform the enforced kowtow to the emperor, the court was amazed and outraged.

Little was known of the *fan-qui*, the "foreign devils" who came from the other side of the world, eager to buy China's teas and silks.

Court officials recognized them instantly as barbarians — universally uncivilized, hirsute and troublesome. "They looked upon trade as their chief occupation," the court noted, "and were wanting in any high purpose."

The Emperor did, however, allow foreigners a brief annual trading season at Canton, in the empire's far south. But the foreign merchants could neither enter the high-walled city nor deal with any of his subjects other than a monopolistic group of similarly despised merchants.

Soon China teas and chinoiserie were enjoying a great vogue in England.

Early Victorians, presiding over silver tea trays, began to express a marked preference for the "new season leaf"

— and the race was on at the shipyards to produce the fast-sailing clippers that would win the best tea prices.

The breathtaking sight of tea clippers in full sail, riding the northeast monsoons on the race to London; the skill of the seamen and the legendary lifestyles of the merchant princes — all added to the romance of the China Trade, and the mystery of the fabled empire that was the source of teas and silks, porcelain and lacquerware.

"What does anybody here know of China?" asked the young British historian Macauley in 1840. "Even those Europeans who have been in that empire are almost as ignorant of it as the rest of us.

"Everything is covered by a veil, through which a glimpse of what is within may occasionally be caught a glimpse just sufficient to set the imagination at work. . ."

Britain's treasury soon realized the price of the nation's indulgence for things Chinese in terms of silver bullion. The Romans had learnt a similar lesson when demand for China's silks had threatened to bankrupt their empire.

British merchants were determined to find merchandise that would balance the trade which — like all dealings with China — was so unequal.

They had to look no further than Britain's latest imperial acquisition — India, with its acres of opium poppies. '

The British East India Company took command and extended the acres of bright poppies, auctioning off the harvest. Opium had been bartered for centuries on the China coast, though the Emperor had forbidden its import.

But a demand for the illicit drug existed, and, desperate to balance the China Trade, the merchants intended to exploit it.

Soon the potent sap, lanced from ripe seedpods, wrapped in red petals, hardened and packed in chests, was feeding the opium dreams of China's addicts.

And the flow of silver bullion to China was balanced; then reversed.

At Whampoa, just below Canton, the European ships anchored to load the teas, silks and porcelain that comprised the legitimate merchandise of the China Trade.

In the Pearl River estuary, close to Portuguese Macau, lay Lintin Island, base for the illegal trade in opium.

During the winter trading season, when the monsoons could give their clippers a speedy start for the voyage to London, the merchants lived in Whampoa warehouses.

In summer they sojourned in Macau, where mistresses and elegant mansions, churches and cobbled streets made them briefly nostalgic for the cities of Europe.

The merchants would entertain their dinner guests with tales of the tantalizing miniature of China their Whampoa base afforded them.

And while the port was passed they savoured stories of the elaborate system of "squeeze" and official deception that enabled Chinese officials to profit from the trade in opium while pacifying the Emperor who forbade it.

Occasionally, when an opium clipper had discharged its cargo, it would be "chased" by Chinese men-of-war junks furiously discharging cannon. The clipper captain, feigning alarm, would fly for the open sea.

And both mandarin and captain would enjoy the spectacle of a masque as colourful as any staged for court entertainment!

However, the Emperor finally determined to stop the trade that was depleting his nation's silver, corrupting his officials and debilitating his subjects — for even his palace eunuchs and bodyguards were addicts.

Edicts were issued in vermilion: "Obey and remain; disobey and depart. Tremble hereat! Intensely tremble! " Opium was confiscated from the merchants, and a cordon of soldiers was drawn around their Whampoa warehouse.

This was just the sort of "insult" British merchants had been waiting for. Victorious in Europe, mistress of an empire, Britain reacted swiftly to this challenge to the nation's "ancient rights of commerce".

With eyes firmly on the flag — rather than the confiscated chests of smuggled opium — Lord Palmerston dispatched frigates, and China's ill-equipped forts were subdued.

The Treaty of Nanking opened four new ports to foreigners and ceded to Britain "a barren island" which, Lord Palmerston scoffed, would never be a mart of trade.

But the Queen was amused.

Victoria Alexandrina, Queen Empress of an empire, was initially as vexed as Palmerston at the lustreless new jewel in her imperial crown. But finally its sheer insignificance made it something of a royal joke.

"Albert is so much amused at my having got the island of Hong Kong," she wrote to her uncle, "and we think Victoria ought to be called Princess of Hong Kong..."

That was in 1841, almost twenty years before the camera began to record the island's embryonic growth.

Prior to the arrival of the British, Hong Kong had slumbered in the South China Sea. Its stern granite crests thrust into the blue sunlit air; the tropical greenery of its sheer flanks dipped deep beneath the water that separated it from the mainland.

Though it failed to arouse the interest of the mandarin in whose province it lay, it had caught the eye of Britain's Lord Napier. Searching for an offshore base for the China Trade merchants, Napier had noted Hong Kong's "safe and commodious harbour".

This sheltered swath of water was approached through a narrow pass that pirates found a convenient ambush point. But pirates apart, it was a safe haven — especially from the great storms unleashed by the monsoons that swept up from the Philippines.

For centuries the island's bays had sheltered fisherfolk who chased shoals across the South China Sea. Later it became a lair for pirates plundering the trading ships that had begun to ply these waters.

Then, as the Dragon had surmised, the missionaries and merchants were followed by scarlet-uniformed soldiers, frigates, sailors — and the flag.

The flag was planted at Possession Point when the wags of Macau were still debating the island's name.

Was it called Hong Kong — Fragrant Harbour — for the scented sandalwood used in its fishing junks; for the

incense it shipped to Canton; or for the sweet mountain streams that cascaded into a bay much favoured as an anchorage?

The British, American and Indian merchants wasted no time in such debates. When Hong Kong's first land auction was held they were only interested in securing their stake on the island Palmerston had so derided.

While some might have harboured regrets at leaving the mellow comfort of their homes on Macau's Praya Grande, the shrewdest were already envisaging the dirt track along the waterfront that would be Queen's Road, and the city that would be called Victoria.

Merchants bid for waterfront lots that would soon accommodate their godowns and private jetties. The Navy secured a site for a permanent dockyard. The Army opted for a hilltop camp and barracks.

The rival taipans of Jardine & Matheson and Dent & Co. — whose clippers had raced across many an ocean — secured both waterfront and residential lots.

Matheson's Point, with its slipway and workshops, would soon be a magnet for rake-masted opium clippers, junks and sampans. Soon visitors would be commending the wine and imported chef at Matheson's Number One House on a tree-shaded hillside overlooking the ocean. And down in the centre of the new town they would marvel at the three acres of exotic flowers and imported plants that were transforming the "barren island" around John Dent's mansion "Green-bank".

In those early days it must have seemed to the Portuguese merchants in Macau that the island was as stubbornly unyielding as the Scottish and Chinese merchants who were transforming its dauntingly craggy face.

No sooner had the townsite been hacked out of granite, and tents, matshed godowns and houses erected, than a typhoon tore up the entire town and scattered its ships across Napier's "safe and commodious" harbour. Five days later the tropical storm returned to demolish the repairs.

The typhoon was followed by fire and fever: the former consuming the matshed homes and stalls of the bazaar; the latter racking the bodies of young men in the army camp who died every day, so very far from home.

But though the headstones on the hillside cemetery multiplied alarmingly — and the merchants of Macau relished each new tale of piracy, robbery, fever or fire — the island evinced an unashamed instinct for survival.

Hong Kong had become one of a galaxy of far-flung imperial islands which would be fashioned into tiny tropical replicas of Victorian England.

Clock towers, cathedral spires and domed civic buildings would attest to the high Victorian moral tone and pride of the young city of Victoria. The fact that many of its fine buildings would be financed by the fortunes of smugglers would not prove a source of agony to the plumed helmets that administered the new colony.

The imperial impulse that had won Britain an empire was born of bold effrontery — to hesitate was to court disaster.

The commercial impulse that took root in the free port of Hong Kong was equally forthright — make a fortune, whatever the price.

Hong Kong's location on China's doorstep assured it an ever-swelling population.

Whenever turmoil convulsed its gigantic neighbour, the island inherited a stream of refugees from famine, flood or rebellion.

The anti-Manchu Taiping Rebellion, which erupted on the mainland in the 1850s, soon spread across the Yangtze Valley. Though it was Christian-based, the movement's high-minded fanatics who outlawed opium and alcohol, foot-binding and prostitution were not averse to slaughter on a large scale.

When the rebels took Nanking and killed the entire 25,000 garrison of soldiers and their families, Hong Kong experienced its first human flood. Farmers, shop-keepers, peasants and coolies — all were seeking refuge from the spreading civil strife.

For the rich merchant settling in Hong Kong there was the chance to open a shop, perhaps selling jade: beautifully-carved ornaments from pale pink to purple; or lucky green finger jades in symbolic shapes — peach for longevity, chicken heart for fertility that people loved to caress.

The Chinese had always valued jade above any other stone, believing it to be a link between heaven and earth, life and immortality. It was said that when the Manchus invaded China — forcing men to wear the pigtails that symbolized submission — the Imperial Dragon shed tears of sorrow that petrified into jade.

Before opening his shop the merchant would consult both a *feng shui* man and a fortune teller.

The *feng shui* "wind and water" man would examine the site of the shop, study the direction of wind and water located nearby dragon spirits, and decide whether its location would adversely affect the *Ch'i*, or spiritual breath of the universe.

If the merchant's new home or shop lay in the direct path of malevolent spirits, the *feng shui* man would advise on strategically placed walls, screens, mirrors or dragon images that could deflect the spirits and protect the occupants.

The fortune teller would consult his ancient almanac, which contained detailed advice on matters ranging from propitious dates for opening a shop to staging a funeral.

In both his home and shop, the merchant would tend the shrine of the God of Wealth, for neglected gods might withdraw their favours or make adverse reports when next visiting heaven. For insurance purposes he might also curry favour with other deities whose shrines were located at the local temple.

The merchant, mindful of filial duty, would also tend the shrines of his ancestors, knowing that when a man died his spirit took triple form: one accompanied the body to the omega-shaped grave on a sheltered hillside; another journeyed to the underworld to encounter again the corrupt officials who had plagued his life; while a third resided in the ancestral tablets preserved in the home or temple.

If all three spirits were not placated by constant attention

they would roam the city inflicting hardship on the living.

While the rich merchant dined with wives and concubines on soups made from sharks' fins and swallows' nests brought from Cochin China and Cambodia and fortified himself with elixirs prepared from the antlers of deer or pickled seaweed, the newly-arrived coolie and his wife would subsist on meagre bowls of rice or millet, flavoured with a trace of fish or vegetable.

But the coolie would not waste time on envy. Like the merchant he would burn joss sticks before the God of Wealth, meanwhile working untold hours a day to secure the fortune he felt sure lay ahead.

For merchant and coolie shared a common philosophy.

Both recognized that man's fortune reflected the dual forces of Yin and Yang, heaven and earth, male and female, light and dark, that balanced the cosmos.

Both were conscious of the inexorable tide of fortune so evident in the tragedies and triumphs that filled the lives of their own ancestors.

Both knew that wealth and power could be snatched away by a fickle fate, and the poor man could rise to take the rich man's place.

It was all a matter of good joss and timing, and living by one's wits.

It was all a philosophy shared by the young colony, balancing the ambitions of China and Britain while nurturing its own.

As the unrest generated by the Taiping Rebellion festered on the mainland, Hong Kong witnessed preparations for war. Britain was determined that the veil concealing the Imperial Dragon should finally be ripped away.

An Anglo-French expeditionary force made camp on the peninsula opposite the island. The rocky ground was cleared, wells dug, roads cut and tents pitched. Soldiers, horses and artillery illustrated the military might of forces that would bombard and occupy Canton, then storm the imperial capital, Peking.

In 1860 an artist with the *London Illustrated News* noted with delight the colour contrasts of British and French troops, and the varying shapes of headgear — huge turbans for the Sikh troops from British India, and helmet shaped pith hats for the British.

"I never saw anything more picturesque than the camp," he observed. "The scenery in itself is beautiful and is rendered doubly so by the varieties of costumes worn by the officers and men."

But the pretty picture of the encamped troops was soon stained by the bloodshed of the war that followed. Though the Chinese troops fought bravely they were no match for the well-equipped foreign armies. Thousands died in battle, and thousands more took their own lives rather than live with the humiliation of the foreign victory.

The human cost of defending the Forbidden City, and the humiliation of seeing the Emperor's fabled Summer Palace looted and burned to the ground by "barbarian" troops had a profound effect on China.

For the plundering foreign troops the Summer Palace — its treasure-filled pavilions, its painted bridges and ornamental lakes and gardens — was a symbol of a dynasty remote from reality.

For the people of China the pall of smoke hanging over the Summer Palace marked another stage in the slow death of the Manchu dynasty.

The treaty that ended hostilities stripped away the last of the restrictions on travel that China had deployed to foreign incursions into the Middle Kingdom.

Foreigners had now won, by war, the right to travel, to evangelize, to trade — to photograph — anywhere in China.

They were even permitted to establish their offices and homes in an extended number of ports which offered extra-territoriality — the protection of their own national laws.

China, once again, paid an indemnity and ceded another slice of territory to the precocious British colony growing apace on its doorstep.

In the high-handed tradition of empire, Britain had already made considerable use of the Kowloon peninsula — to accommodate troops for the allied expeditionary force — before it was ceded as part of the Treaty of Peking in 1860.

When the government held the first public auction of Kowloon's "garden lots" it clearly saw the recumbent peninsula as a place for market gardens, orchards and the prize-winning chrysanthemums a local tycoon would soon be nurturing.

But the businessmen who secured the peninsula's waterfront lots weren't thinking of pretty gardens, but of wharves and warehouses.

In the early days the wharves jutting out into Hong Kong's harbour were privately owned by companies such as Jardine, Matheson and the P & O Line.

Cargo was unloaded by sweating coolies, heaving bales and boxes from the holds of ships to the junks clustered below.

Meanwhile great ports like London and Liverpool were building networks of wharves that cut labour costs, damage to goods and a vessel's turnaround time in port.

Always quick to learn such lessons, the colony's front-runners — Matheson, Dent, Chater and Sassoon — began planning dock companies, wooden wharves, cranes, trolleys and turntables.

Though a complex web of trade soon linked the colony with the capitals of the world, opium still loomed large as a source of wealth. Hong Kong had become a convenient port at which opium from India could be transferred to vessels adapted for the coastal trade of China. In its early years, three-quarters of the Indian opium crop passed through the port, much of it in the P & O Line ships operating in the Far East.

Although it had now won the right to trade in additional Chinese ports, Britain did not undertake to stop the opium trade, which was now satisfying the addiction of two million Chinese.

To prohibit the cultivation and export of the drug would both destabilize the economy of British India and drastically reduce Hong Kong's revenue.

A far better solution was to avert the official eye.

One of the colony's first governors, Sir Henry Pottinger, had announced that his administration would offer no protection to opium adventurers and, like the Chinese Emperor, their cargo.

But the shrewd Scot Matheson, writing to his partner, had explained: "I believe it is like the Chinese edicts, meaning nothing, and only meant for the saints in England.

"Sir Henry never means to act on it, and no doubt privately considers it a good joke. At any rate he allows the drug to be landed and stored at Hong Kong."

And when the trade became legal it would even be shown off, with a hint of colonial pride. Queen Victoria's grandsons would one day watch the unloading of opium in Hong Kong's harbour.

Later they would pronounce the colony "a little England in the Eastern seas, a creation of British energy, enterprise and industry."

To the Victorian traveller Hong Kong offered an amalgam of experiences every bit as intoxicating as the cocktail — laced with tobacco juice and arsenic — that foreign sailors enjoyed on the Canton waterfront.

By the 1870s the colony boasted all the comforts and entertainments esteemed by mid-Victorian society in an outpost of empire.

But Hong Kong mixed its Victorian refinement with the enticing fizz of smuggling and piracy — and this guaranteed its inclusion in the itinerary of English globe-trotters like Miss Isabella Bird, who visited in 1878.

The arrival of a steamship was announced by the sounding of a gun and the hoisting of a flag on the island's highest point.

From the granite Peak, tropical greenery fell sheer to the lower levels of gleaming white porticoes, church spires and hillside temples.

The steamer's hull was soon surrounded by bucking sampans and the raucous shouts of women thrusting up armfuls of silks, fans and trinkets.

Beyond them, sinewy coolies loaded cargoes of tea, cotton, silver bullion and coal. One clipper ship might be loading pre-cut granite blocks destined to build a goldtown in California; another might have arrived with Alaskan ice, wrapped in straw, to cool the colonists' food chests.

At the pier there were sedan chairs for hire, and Miss Isabella Bird secured one on arrival.

"A bamboo chair, with two lean coolies, carried me at a swinging pace through streets as steep as those of Genoa," she would write.

"Most of its streets are so steep as to be impassable for wheeled vehicles, and some are merely great flights of stairs arched over by dense foliaged trees...

It has green balconies with festoons of creepers, lofty houses, people and costumes of all nations, processions of Portuguese priests and nuns.

All its many-coloured life is seen to full advantage under this blue sky and brilliant sun."

Miss Bird saw ivy-covered mansions that might have been transplanted from her native England; a Gothic-styled Bishop's Palace; gracefully arcaded Victorian buildings; and porcelain-tiled Chinese rooftops on which undulating dragons halted the approach of malevolent spirits.

Houses climbed the lower flanks of the Peak, and stood behind beautiful balustrading, on massive stone retaining walls that were already sprouting tropical ferns.

Travellers soon appreciated that in Hong Kong people loved to make a show. Every member of a wealthy family would have a sedan chair, and when ladies took their evening promenade along the few miles of carriage road they would insist their chairs and bearers followed — at a discreet distance, of course! The Governor's sedan was instantly recognizable — its eight bearers in scarlet livery with white gaiters and round felt hats topped with scarlet tassels.

A tour of the city centre acquainted the visitor with its court, hotels, post office, shops and the impressive City Hall complex with its library, museum, hall, ballroom and theatre. Its building was largely financed by Jardine, Matheson; the water fountain that graced its forecourt was a gift from Dent & Co.

On the south side of Queen's Road stood the handsome three-storey Hong Kong Club. The Club was all fluted columns, crystal chandeliers, leather armchairs and softly padding servants. Just the sort of place to make "the right sort of people" feel at home — and others excluded, and irritated!

Chinese flower-sellers outside The Club soon realized that members could be cajoled into buying a buttonhole, particularly when the Kowloon garden lots made the blooms cheaper. As business flourished the flower-sellers spread further up Wyndham — or Flower — Street. They shaded their bright baskets beneath spreading banyan trees.

In fact the island itself was losing its "barren" face as luxuriant shrubbery began to encircle and embroider roads and public buildings.

In the new public gardens visitors were constantly surprised by the recently-imported trees and shrubs, as they promenaded to the strains of the military band.

Regimental bands also accompanied the horse races at Happy Valley.

Soon after the colony's foundation a mosquito-infested valley was drained and levelled, and realists surmised it

was not so much the fever as a desire for a racecourse that spurred the project.

The annual Chinese New Year races proved an equal lure to all residents from labourers to taipans. The latter entertained lavishly in refreshment booths stocked with pigeon pie, game, cold joints, preserves, champagne and stout, while betting heavily on China ponies from the great Mongolian plains that trainers claimed had "fire in their hearts". These small ponies had crossed the Gobi desert to be auctioned to dealers in China, and they raced alongside ponies from the Philippines and Australia.

From the grandstand the view was breathtaking — the embrace of green hills, the glitter of service uniforms, the

sheen of Chinese silks and the sweating flanks of the flying ponies.

The Times's China correspondent would describe it thus: "The Londoner cannot conceive the excitement caused in this little distant island by the race week which is the single holiday of the merchants. They spend weighty sums on importing horses from all parts and training them for the contest.

When first we see the racecourse in Happy Valley we are half tempted to declare it the most picturesque spot in the world..."

The racecourse, parade ground, barracks, cricket and polo grounds, all lying to the east of the city, were the

domain of plumed helmets, taipans and swaggering subalterns.

To the west lay the Chinese shops for foreigners, the solid brick square of Western Market, and the crowded, noisy, insanitary network of alleys filled with shops, teahouses and stalls that was the Chinese section of the segregated town.

Into this area plumed helmets seldom ventured, so that when plague erupted in the 1890s officials were horrified at the overcrowded conditions in which both humans and animals lived.

In this section of town the day began before dawn with the distinctive call of the congee hawker offering breakfasts of fish, barley, kidney or pork congee. Like so many hawkers he carried his kitchen on his back — two baskets suspended from a shoulder pole.

The narrow dirt roads were full of jostling shoppers all haggling over the price of lotus roots or squares of bean curd, golden mangoes or flattened amber ducks.

In the evening the area glowed with lanterns.

Boys played with kites and old men walked their singing birds, showing off fancy cages and porcelain waterbowls.

Pretty girls coiled and ornamented their sleek black hair, and old women lit long-stemmed pipes and opened fans.

The shrill pipe and gong of a street opera troupe announced the start of an evening performance.

In crowded courtyards the smoke of cooking fires mingled with the incense of shrines. Cobblers, black-smiths, tinkers, coffin-makers, barbers, fortune-tellers, merchants and coolies crouched over flickering candles and rice bowls.

On Christmas night in 1878, a fire broke out in this area, destroying property on Queen's Road plus a large area of slums.

Miss Isabella Bird was assured by a fellow passenger that it was no use going ashore, for half the town had burned down.

She went anyway, and watched firemen and residents frantically fighting the blaze and trying to salvage their worldly goods. She recalled: "Men belonging to the insurance companies running out with drawn swords, miscellaneous police running hither and thither... heavy crashes as of tottering walls, and above all the loud bell of the Romish cathedral tolling rapidly."

The fire raged through the night, and Constance

Cummings provided another eyewitness account of its devastation in "Wanderings in China": "For seventeen hours the fire raged on with unabated might, till it made a clean sweep of about four hundred houses, covering about ten acres of ground, and leaving thousands of poor creatures homeless...

I never could have believed that any community could have borne so awful a calamity so bravely and patiently... Not a tear have I seen shed."

In the Chinese section of town the contrasts that characterised Hong Kong were equally evident.

In dank corners of fetid courtyards, humans and animals crowded together in a few square feet of living space.

Behind high walls topped with gold and green tiles, rich merchants entertained in marble-floored reception rooms furnished with the rigid formality of carved blackwood.

The wealthy merchant was surrounded by women who seldom ventured out unless concealed behind the silken curtains of a hurrying palanquin.

The merchant's wives, and his string of concubines, were proud of their beribboned "golden lily" feet, forcibly compressed since childhood to the crippling five inches that titillated men.

Though initially designed to discourage women from straying, the ploy was less than successful, for foot-binding became an erotic attribute in itself — and at least one Hong Kong Governor was surprised by a delegation of merchants appealing that their runaway concubines should be made punishable under English law!

The growth of trade throughout China had gradually changed the status of the merchant, once considered on a humble par with actors in the hierarchy of Chinese society.

The compradors — who acted as intermediaries between foreign companies and local traders — won generous commissions from the taipans who employed them, and an enviable social status in the colony.

With his impeccable silks and swansdown fans, Robert Ho Tung, who joined Jardine, Matheson as a shipping clerk in 1880, was destined to become the colony's most famous comprador. He married into the firm, and when his English wife could bear no children took a second wife who produced ten. During sixty-seven years with the company he amassed a fortune and would eventually be knighted.

Such men were a link between the old and new patterns of trade in China, and between the Oriental and Western worlds that coexisted in Hong Kong.

The compradors were the first Chinese given the social accolade of an invitation to Government House by Sir Arthur Kennedy in the 1870s. In doing so the governor incurred the wrath of the British merchants, for Government House symbolized the peak of high society in Hong Kong.

Kennedy was the first governor to break the social maxim enunciated by an earlier governor who felt it his duty to "preserve the European and American community from the injury and inconvenience" of mixing with the Chinese.

The colony's social and residential segregation was to be further challenged by Kennedy's successor, Sir John

Pope Hennessy.

Rumours of the new governor's sympathy for the "subject races" of empire had preceded his arrival in 1877. It was said that planters had protested his policies as a colonial governor from Barbados to Labuan.

In the latter, a fever-infested island off Borneo, Pope Hennessy had met and married his wife Kitty, who was half his age and very beautiful. Kitty was the daughter of Sir Hugh Low, who had aspired to be governor of Labuan before Pope Hennessy's appointment. A strain of Malay blood was evident in Kitty's striking eyes and silken dark hair, and the turbulent early years of her marriage had kept the Labuan Club well fuelled with gossip.

From the moment Pope Hennessy stepped ashore in Hong Kong with the moody, mercurial Kitty, his policies, her beauty — and the passions both inspired — were staples of conversation whenever cigar smoke curled above leather armchairs.

First the new governor criticized the nine o'clock curfew, after which no Chinese was allowed on the streets without a pass and a lantern. Then he proceeded to suspend flogging, branding and the deportation of criminals.

British residents, inured to sleeping with revolvers at the ready, considered all these measures essential in fighting a level of crime that was as endemic to Hong Kong as opium smuggling.

By the 1870s Chinese firms were moving aggressively to the forefront of the colony's trade, and settling in the Central district, hitherto a European preserve.

The enlightened new governor gave them his full support, actively opposing discrimination and helping to raise the status of the whole Chinese community.

The result was that Pope Hennessy won the accolade "Number One Friend" from Chinese residents, and his reforms brought an influx of Chinese settlers from the mainland.

Some came to establish businesses that broadened the base of the Chinese community.

Others came to seek a more sympathetic working environment — for the punishments and tortures meted out to criminals on the mainland were ingeniously horrid.

With the crime rate spiralling, meetings of the Legislative Council, previously unnoticed by the population, became the substance of heated debates, particularly after the governor appointed the first Chinese councillor — an articulate and wealthy barrister.

Pope Hennessy, the fiery Irishman, seemed to thrive on controversy, but it was conflict in his private, not public, life that brought about his demise in Hong Kong.

On a mountain road near his Peak summer lodge, the governor allegedly attacked — with his umbrella — an eminent British barrister who, it was whispered, had been enamoured by Kitty's dark eyes.

Soon after Sir James and Kitty departed for another colonial posting on another tropical island. They were farewelled by many Chinese residents, but not a single foreign merchant.

Pope Hennessy had entirely lived up to his reputation as

"the stormy petrel of the Colonial Service".

There was another sort of storm in the 1870s — a typhoon which hit Hong Kong one evening and was at its height by midnight.

Residents in the town's upper levels could hear, above the din of the storm, the anguished shrieks from the harbour as sampans and junks were smashed and steamers were hurled like sledgehammers into the praya walls.

Next morning each wrecked vessel was surrounded by drifting bodies, for two thousand had lost their lives in six terrible hours.

But Hong Kong was well used to picking itself up, rebuilding and improving what had been destroyed. And there was always an opportunist who would turn disaster into gain.

Paul Chater, an Armenian, came to Hong Kong in 1864 at the age of 18 and within a decade had made a fortune as an exchange and bullion broker.

Chater had always envisaged a row of deep-water wharves along the Kowloon waterfront. When the typhoon of 1874 ruined one group of businessmen, Chater turned his visionary eye on their battered waterfront lots. The wharf, godown and cargo company he launched later merged with Matheson's wharf interests to become one of the colony's principal commercial docks.

The Armenian, descended from princes, had an unerring instinct for making a fortune. Not only did he turn a handsome profit from Hong Kong's real estate, he conceived its extension through the government's most ambitious reclamation project — which added a slice of land two miles long to the city's heart.

Hong Kong loved a success story. Tales of Chater's phenomenal wealth — his stables of race horses, his stately mansion "Marble Hall" — added to his mystique and fed the ambition of other fortunehunters.

And the colony's early decades were to produce many such stories.

Douglas Lapraik, who arrived in the 1840s, started his Hong Kong career as a watchmaker's assistant. Thirteen years later he owned docks, his own shipping company, the Douglas Steamship Company and his own miniature Douglas Castle overlooking the ocean.

Equally enticing was the tale of a Parsee who arrived as a cook and ended up a prosperous hotelier — Dorabjee Nowrojee's King Edward Hotel was acknowledged as one of the best in town. He was also the founder of Hong Kong's most famous form of transport — the Star Ferry.

After the Evening Star began making harbour crossings in 1897, a Chinese businessman, Lau Tak Po, bought five wooden boats, turned them into ferries and began services to areas of Kowloon not served by the Star Ferry.

He soon owned four steam-driven steel ferries, and his Hong Kong and Yaumati Ferry Company was destined to become the largest Chinese-owned company in the world.

The vision and instinct which added to a tycoon's mystique were only part of any success story. The other was born of attitude — being flexible enough to embrace new patterns of trade, adopt new skills and

exploit new technologies.

The colony had lived through a financial crisis in the 1860s which claimed many companies, including Dent & Co. The advent of steam and the electric telegraph and the opening of the Suez and Panama canals would all change the way in which business was conducted.

Companies like Jardine, Matheson moved into new areas: establishing cotton mills in Shanghai, building railways and selling military equipment to China. The company was also quick to utilize the electric telegraph, the first line in China being erected between its East Point and Central offices. Cable services connecting Hong Kong with Shanghai, New York, London and

Southeast Asia followed.

Besides trading on its own account, Hong Kong was benefiting from the growth of trade within China. By the 1880s it was handling twenty-one percent of China's exports, thirty-seven percent of her imports.

Shipping companies from across the world opened offices in Hong Kong, and industries linked with trade — shipbuilding and repairing — also flourished.

The colony had built its first ship at a private shipyard in 1843 . Soon it was producing an array of vessels from customs vessels to gunboats. Its customers included the Spanish government in the Philippines and the Chinese Navy.

By the turn of the century Hong Kong could build ships faster than any competitor; was challenging Britain's supremacy in this field, and, with a population of only 300,000, had become the world's second largest port.

In the latter part of the 19th century, Hong Kong's harbour offered Chinese emigrants a last glimpse of China as they embarked on steamers destined for foreign shores.

Chinese emigrants were prepared to go wherever there was a demand for labour, to work on mines, plantations or goldfields. Some went as free emigrants; others were kidnapped and shipped as human cargo; many went as contract labour. For the latter the work was hard, the pay minimal and the conditions on vessels so bad that many died during the voyage.

Though the British Government finally prohibited the shipping of contract labour, Hong Kong remained an important centre for emigration.

More than two hundred Chinese, most returning from the Californian goldfields, were deck passengers on a Douglas Steamship vessel which left Hong Kong for Swatow in December of 1890.

The ship's British captain was just sitting down to tiffin with his five saloon passengers when the boat was intercepted and attacked by fifty Chinese pirates brandishing cutlasses and revolvers.

The ship was looted. Everything of value disappeared over the horizon with the pirated vessel, and four, including the captain, were left dead.

So the deck passengers, who had gone to California to build goldtowns in the wilderness, returned to China empty-handed but lucky to be alive.

The attack was typical of the times, for in the late 19th

century Hong Kong was a magnet for pirates who were every bit as bloodthirsty as those of the Barbary Coast.

At least two of the fleets were commanded by foreigners — the renegade Englishman William Fenton and the American Eli Boggs.

Both had eluded British, Chinese and Portuguese naval vessels for years. When Fenton's pirate lorcha was finally seized he leapt overboard, but was fished out to face the courts.

Fenton and Boggs ended up in jail, and were fortunate compared to the brigands and pirates captured on the mainland. Brigands were slowly lowered into vats of lime; pirates were decapitated.

"April 17, 1891, was a day of blood..." read the *Hong Kong Telegraph*, describing a mass execution that took place on the boundary between British and Chinese Kowloon. The pirates, hands bound, chained by the neck, knelt in line on the beach as the executioner advanced with his heavy iron sword.

"Standing over the first man the executioner lifted the crude weapon above his head, there was a flash and the head fell to the ground... On and on went the butcher, performing his dreadful work so efficiently that the scene almost lost its terror. . . Several Europeans crossed over from Hong Kong to witness the execution."

White was the symbolic colour of death in China.

Coffin bearers garbed in white had to make their grief conspicuous to appease the departed. In the past a two-year mourning was observed, but it shortened as the pace of life accelerated.

Old-timers complained there was no time for the dead.

Government officials soon discovered there was no place for the dying.

Because of traditional beliefs that death should not occur in the family home, and the time and place of burial should be dictated by *feng shui*, it soon became apparent that Chinese temples had become death houses for the poor.

The Surveyor General had been horrified to discover within a temple "the dead and dying huddled together indiscriminately in small filthy rooms".

This discovery prompted the establishment of the Tung Wah Hospital, which became a powerful force in the Chinese community.

At that time there was no law requiring Chinese to

register deaths but, despite this, in May of 1894 it was noticed that a terrible fever was spreading through the narrow, insanitary streets of Victoria's worst slum.

By the end of the month four hundred and fifty were dead. Two months later it was two thousand.

There was widespread distrust of Western medicine, and when government officials began removing the sick and dying, disinfecting and evacuating fever-stricken slums, they intruded on the all-important rituals surrounding death and burial.

Anger spread as rapidly as the fever.

Schools emptied; trade was affected when Hong Kong was declared an infected port; thousands fled to the

mainland; and when by-laws relating to the disposal of the dead were passed, the dead and dying were smuggled from one filthy alley to the next.

As the toll mounted, so did resentment.

The authorities were blamed for not having acted when fever stories filtered from Canton. Chinese doctors claimed their treatment of fever victims was as effective as the brandy and ice-packs recommended by Western doctors. The Tung Wah Hospital demanded responsibility for all the Chinese plague victims, while British doctors accused it of fostering anti-foreign feeling.

Meanwhile a Japanese doctor took up residence in the slums of Tai Ping Shan, where thousands had been turned

out of their homes.

Professor Kitasato collected the dead bodies of rats, and his research finally isolated the plague bacillus in 1894.

The colony's British medical officer considered his findings absurd, as did the local English newspapers.

But the people listened to Professor Kitasato's advice not to drink unsterilized water or eat uncooked food. By July the death toll had eased, the temporary plague hospitals began to close and trade picked up.

People filtered back from the mainland to the congested, temporarily disinfected streets of Tai Ping Shan — the "Hill of the Great Peace".

In the late 1880s artists were sculpting hundreds of statues of a rotund British matron destined to sit in far-flung outposts of empire, shaded from the noon-day sun by canopies of granite or marble.

Hong Kong's Great White Queen was fashioned by Raggio in bronze, and when it was unveiled amid the pomp and circumstance of Victoria's jubilee in 1887, the "subject races" were amused to note that the bronze face of the Empress was as dark as her widow's weeds. . .

Victoria was as remote a figure to her Hong Kong subjects as the extraordinary Empress who ruled China at the time from behind the twenty-foot high walls of Peking's Forbidden City.

The Dowager Empress Tzu Hsi, once an imperial concubine, had assumed power by eliminating both an empress and a son who threatened her autocratic rule as regent. She then nurtured a nephew for the Dragon Throne, but imprisoned him when he evinced a zeal for reform. She would remain in power until her death in 1908.

Surrounded by eunuchs, palace guards, court musicians and the lakes and gardens of the Forbidden City, the Empress had little grasp of the world beyond.

She had no central treasury, just an array of provincial viceroys and governors who bolstered the imperial coffers whenever threatened. Corruption was rife, but when a dishonest official was exposed, the empress seemed more interested in acquiring his confiscated treasure than eradicating the cancer that was eroding Manchu authority.

When advised of Japan's modern navy and acquisitive overtures, the empress agreed to modernize the Chinese Imperial Navy, then diverted much of the foreign loan intended for national "self-strengthening" to build herself another summer palace.

When war with Japan broke out in 1894, China suffered a decisive defeat, ceded more tertitory and paid another crippling war indemnity.

The Dowager Empress was aware of the slow seeping of Western knowledge — of finance, technology, science, history and, most important, of republican constitutional government. When a group of young reformers gained access to her nephew, she acted swiftly to imprison him.

But though the Manchu dynasty refused to move with the times, the new knowledge took root in the minds of the young, some studying abroad — like Sun Yat Sen in Hong Kong — others travelling far beyond the nation they once considered the centre of civilization.

Tzu Hsi was also aware of the groundswell of anti-foreign sentiment, which was as strong as the anti-Manchu movements gaining strength in the provinces. When the Boxer Rebellion broke out in 1899 she supported the attacks on Chinese Christians and Europeans.

The rebellion saw the eruption of resentment that had grown as China was being bled bankrupt by the indemnities each foreign victory extracted. China had been defeated by the British, French and Japanese, and each victorious nation had helped to dismantle the Chinese empire: Japan taking Korea and Taiwan; Russia occupying Manchuria; the British taking Burma and the French Vietnam.

On its own territory, China was forced to make concessions to foreign powers that were slicing it into "spheres of influence" and squabbling over railway and mining rights.

The once proud people of China watched, seemingly powerless.

But the new knowledge was already at work.

Rebellion and revolution tore at the fabric of society, scattering silk to reveal home spun, as China lurched into the 20th century...

One of the territorial leases China was forced to concede added to Hong Kong's embrace the mountains, valleys and islands of the New Territories.

The mainland area had been little changed by the unhurried centuries.

Swallows came south each year to nest under the eaves of ancestral halls. Gaudily clad gods gazed from hillside temples on to valleys that changed colour with each season. Patient women planted row after row of seedling rice in muddy-brown paddies, then tender green shoots deepened to emerald and the gold of harvest.

But village life had not always been peaceful, for this area of walled clan villages was home to Cantonese farmers whose fierce feuds had often been a source of annoyance to the Viceroy in Canton. However, when the British took control of the area in 1899 the clans united in a brief but spirited resistance.

In the New Territories' bays clustered the craft of Hoklo and Tanka fisherfolk. It was said the Tanka had been exiled to the ocean for plotting against a Sung dynasty emperor. It was decreed the Tanka's descendants should never again live on land, so the sea gypsies counted the seasons not by the changes in the landscape but by the passage of shoals.

They returned to land only to anchor their boats, mend their nets and market their catch. Of necessity their floating cities became self-sufficient — families lived, gave birth and died in tiny sampans and weather-worn junks.

The waters around Hong Kong had always been a popular fishing ground for the Tanka. Some formed permanent fishing communities in the bays of Hong Kong island, and along the coastline and islands that comprised the colony's New Territories.

The new seventeen-mile frontier between Hong Kong and China passed through the border village of Lo Wu, and it was through this village that the Kowloon-Canton Railway passed in 1911.

Both the railway and the territory it raced through were additional assets to Hong Kong at a time when the Viceroy of Canton was predicting the colony's eclipse. Canton was preparing to dredge the Pearl River to develop Whampoa as a deep-water port to rival Hong Kong.

It had been the tea trade at Whampoa that had given birth to Hong Kong at a time when the merchant princes still lived in Macau. The Portuguese colony had once been a thriving base for the China trade, but was soon eclipsed by its more aggressive British colonial neighbour.

Macau now decayed elegantly behind pastel shutters and ornamental facades, providing Hong Kong with a spectre of failure that would always haunt the colony.

Hong Kong would never fail to compete or to exploit its assets to the full.

So it kept a wary eye on Whampoa — and remembered forgotten Macao — as it hurtled into the 20th century.

The century's early years found Hong Kong relishing the convenience afforded by electric lights, trams and a cable car — the Peak Tram.

The privileged few permitted residence on the Peak were now carried to its summit in fifteen minutes, and would then board their sedans for the further journey home.

The front seat of the Peak Tram was always reserved for the Governor, who had accorded the Peak its desirable social status by building a summer retreat in addition to the neo-classical Government House down in the city.

Mountain Lodge was a spectacular hilltop eyrie, approached through manicured gardens.

When Sir Frederick Lugard and his wife arrived in 1907, Lady Lugard would long remember the mountain road to the lodge. Scarlet-clad bearers carried her sedan through air which "grew cooler every minute". She glimpsed breathtaking vistas of ocean and islands, then passed through "a beautifully kept English garden" with shaven lawns, tennis courts and flowering shrubs.

She disembarked at a flight of steps leading to a porch and "a cool brown wood hall where the house servants, drawn up on either side, were awaiting their new masters".

Lady Lugard was charmed, but the new governor was less impressed. Like many of his predecessors, Sir Henry loathed the moist clouds that clung to the mountain's upper reaches.

"Damp worse than Nigeria in the rains," he would

complain. "Envelopes all glued together; cigars like bits of sponge!"

While Lugard was governor, he had weightier issues than humidity to contend with.

Finally a concerted international effort was being made to suppress the opium trade which had once dominated the colony's economy and was still, in 1908, worth £5million annually.

In 1891 the trade's opponents had successfully lobbied the British Parliament for a resolution condemning it, and in 1909 an International Opium Conference held in Shanghai further consolidated international opposition.

In 1906 an imperial edict in China gave addicts a decade in which to break their habit. Meanwhile the British Government agreed to reduce exports of opium from India to China by one-tenth each year from 1907, so the trade would be abolished within a decade.

The Hong Kong Government ordered the closure of all the colony's opium divans in 1908.

By that time the companies that had made their first fortunes from smuggling at Lintin Island had become international concerns — building railways, establishing industries and selling arsenals of modern weapons to strengthen the nation that had once isolated them at a winter trading post near Canton.

In 1912 the arrival in Hong Kong of Lugard's successor, Sir Henry May, was symbolic of the troubled times in China.

The previous year Manchu rule had finally collapsed, bringing to an end a 268-year-old dynasty. When Dr Sun Yat Sen proclaimed the Chinese Republic the shaven heads and pigtails, symbol of Manchu domination, disappeared overnight.

But the central government's hold was tenuous, as power-hungry warlords seized control in several provinces.

The lawlessness, which heralded a long period of upheaval in China, spilled over into Hong Kong. As Sir Henry and Lady May, the new Governor and his wife, stepped ashore in Hong Kong, an assassin levelled his revolver and fired.

The bullet splintered the bamboo frame of Lady May's chair, prompting Sir Henry to rise, brush down his coat, cast a contemptuous glance at his assailant, who had been set upon by the crowd, and proceed to a more civil reception at the City Hall.

Conflict on a global scale followed with the outbreak of

World War I. With relative peace in the Pacific, Hong Kong could do little more than raise money for the war effort — and service the twenty-two thousand ships that made use of a harbour far from the dust and smoke of war.

But the peace talks at Versailles were to have dramatic repercussions for China and Hong Kong. The Chinese delegates at Versailles hoped that Western support would help it regain territory snatched by Japan, but the cynical self-interest of imperialist powers at the peace conference served to fan China's interest in communism and the Soviet Union. The stage was set for the civil war that would divide the country until World War II.

China's new nationalism, its criticism of the "unequal

treaties" that had forced it to concede territory, and its opposition to foreign economic domination were all elements that heightened tension between Britain and China.

In 1925 a boycott of British and Japanese goods was organized by the Kuomintang in Canton. This was followed by a general strike by Chinese workers in Hong Kong.

But the strike and the world trade slump that followed failed to cripple Hong Kong. Its harbour was now accommodating a record number of trading vessels, some now carrying merchandise produced in the colony's fledgling industries.

China's torment — the flooding of its rivers, the excesses of its battling warlords — simply ensured a new surge of

refugee labour for the newly-established factories.

The seamen's strike of 1922, which spread to include domestic servants, did provide a few catering headaches at Government House, busy preparing to welcome another royal visitor — the Prince of Wales.

With a staff of only two, and everyone at the end of their tenuous tethers, the Governor was relieved to hear from the Prince's equerry, Louis Mountbatten, that the royal visitor loathed lengthy banquets.

He requested a banquet of not more than four courses, and expressed a fervent wish for a game of polo .

The Prince's visit was just one of many "brilliant occasions" savoured by local press society columns. As business boomed and the cosmopolitan community grew, so did Hong Kong's reputation as a lavish hostess.

In the 1930s it seemed that everyone did business in Hong Kong, and good business had to be celebrated at a ten-course Chinese banquet, or a private reception at a leading hotel.

Hong Kong now boasted a string of grand hotels.

For the romantic there was the verandah of the Repulse Bay Hotel with its mountain backdrop and apron of blue. At sunset the bay took on the colours of the sky and at nightfall glowed with the lanterns of hundreds of fishing boats.

For the ritzy, there was the lobby at the Peninsula, where tycoons and travellers sipped pink gins and stengahs among pillars and palms and ornamental gilt. On the day it opened in 1928 an American visitor said: " I'd feel rich here if I hadn't a dime in my bag". Everyone knew what she meant, and the lobby of "The Pen" quickly became a favourite rendezvous.

But beyond the gilt lobby, the talk was turning to the mounting chaos on the mainland.

Chiang Kai Shek had purged the Kuomintang of its communist supporters; Mao Tse Tung had gathered the remnants of his peasant army for the Long March to Yunan. And exploiting the internal troubles of its neighbour, Japan seized Manchuria and, by 1937, was plunged into war with China. The Japanese would later refer to this period in their history as "the dark valley" — a time when all that was fine and humane in the Japanese soul suffered eclipse.

As Japan swept down China and occupied Canton, Hong Kong shuddered at rumours of the military build-up beyond the paddy fields and duck farms of the New Territories.

Already its tenements, hillsides and temporary shelters were jam-packed with hundreds of thousands of refugees who had fled the machine gun and bayonet.

Hong Kong had been assured it was an "impregnable fortress" like its colonial sister, Singapore. Winston Churchill himself had dismissed the possibility of a Japanese attack on Singapore as remote — "Nothing could be more foolish from their point of view," he had boomed. So Hong Kong took heart, and did not dwell on details like the meagre and outdated military hardware at its disposal should Churchill be proved wrong.

When half the world was gripped in war in 1941, Hong Kong blithely threw the last and longest party of the empire.

On the eve of invasion a lobby group of lonely expatriate husbands was protesting the government's "sensationalist" evacuation of British women and children to Australia, which irritatingly refused to import their amahs.

Japanese agents were abandoning hairdressing salons, massage parlours and bars patronized by British officers and heading for home with an incredible dossier of military information.

Breathless socialites were noting in diaries the Diamond Jubilee Ball of Sir Robert and Lady Ho Tung — the Governor would be there and all the Ho Tung ladies would dazzle guests with their traditional Chinese dress; the bomber fund's "Tin Hat Ball"; the war fund's Christmas Bazaar; Saturday racing at Happy Valley; and a war effort Fancy Dress Ball... all in that frantic final week before invasion.

The ballroom at the Peninsula was ablaze as Japanese bombers streaked over Pearl Harbour. The press dubbed it another "brilliant occasion", and people were reading about it over breakfast tables on Monday, December 8, when thirty planes leapt out of a cloudless winter sky.

Within minutes Hong Kong's antiquated airforce had been wiped out.

When planes filled the sky, locals thought the long-awaited airforce reinforcements had arrived — until they began to empty their bombs.

The planes were followed by a battle-hardened force of Japanese infantry, cavalry, tanks and artillery.

When Hong Kong's mainland territory was lost, a miniature Dunkirk of destroyers and ferries carried soldiers and civilians beyond the deadly rain of shells and mortars — to the island.

General Maltby, commander of the British forces, concentrated all his remaining forces on the island and the BBC announced to the world that Hong Kong was prepared for "an old-fashioned siege". It had refused to surrender.

Lieut General Takashi Sakai had used two divisions to take the mainland, reserving his crack third division in readiness for the island's invasion.

On the night of December 18, following days of relentless shelling and bombing, Japanese troops landed. In that week before Christmas they turned the island into a slaughterhouse, beheading and bayoneting prisoners,

raping nurses and thousands of civilians, and butchering the wounded.

Soon the whole island seemed consumed by fire and smoke and the horrendous roar of bombs and mortars. Battles raged in narrow streets strewn with corpses; across mountains dotted with hillside villas, and on the battlements of a Chinese millionaire's ivy-clad castle where soldiers were bayoneted, beheaded or shot — and tossed into the bay once gazed on by the romantic at sunset.

In the Repulse Bay Hotel, the battle-weary and wounded and frightened gathered as the cordon of war closed around them. By flickering candles they watched nearby hillsides flare, gauged the advance of gunfire and saw ornate ceiling mouldings shatter across plush carpets.

When a guest discerned camouflaged figures in the hotel garden, she hoped they were the advance party of Chiang Kai Shek's promised army, but acknowledged a more likely prospect. "I don't know if you are aware," she told the manageress, "but there are about thirty Japanese soldiers in the hotel gardens..." The manageress promised to do something about it.

Churchill cabled the Governor, Sir Mark Young, urging that resistance be maintained so that the enemy "should be compelled to expend the utmost life and equipment".

But the roads were littered with corpses, fires raged, looters were ransacking the town, and the soldiers — Londoners, Scots, Indians and Canadians, joined by a volunteer force of bankers, clerks and businessmen — had fought non-stop for seventeen days.

On the afternoon of Christmas Day, General Maltby informed Sir Mark Young that the colony could fight no longer. Fifteen minutes later the order to surrender was given to all commanding officers and the white flag went up on Government House.

In the grey of the winter evening, the Governor and the general crossed the harbour that had become a graveyard of crippled vessels, to formally surrender to Lieut General Sakai.

Following the brief ceremony at the Peninsula, the Governor was imprisoned in room 336 and the Japanese set up temporary headquarters in the hotel they would soon rename the Toa Hotel. The Japanese Navy established its base in the plush HongKong Hotel, while the solid granite of the Hongkong and Shanghai Banking Corporation became the headquaters of the Japanese civil administration.

Expatriate soldiers and civilians would be herded into an internment camp at Stanley. As food supplies in the colony ran low, thousands of Chinese would be forced back across the border. Some of the Chinese and Indians who remained in the colony throughout occupation would be able to send their imprisoned colleagues occasional food parcels to vary their mainly rice diet.

Within a matter of weeks, Singapore fell and Japan was master of the Far Eastern seas.

When Hong Kong's new Japanese Governor arrived in February of 1942 he announced at the Toa Hotel: "There is no question that Hong Kong belongs to Japan, but consideration will be given to the Chinese in the way of administration, which will be based on the new order of Greater East Asia, and that means prosperity for all . . . "

The Governor, Lieut General Rensuke Isogai, didn't fancy his chances of survival in a Government House severely weakened by an air-raid tunnel constructed beneath it by the British.

He therefore rebuilt Government House as an architectural amalgam of East and West. Being a master of the tea ceremony, his own suite reflected his passion, and boasted raised floors and Shoji screens.

But even while the Governor was ordering a landscape gardener from Kyoto, an interior designer from Osaka, the British War Office and the Colonial Office in London were setting up a Hong Kong Planning Unit to prepare for the day when the British would re-occupy the colony.

Meanwhile in Stanley Internment Camp there were those who refused to wait. In overcrowded rooms, plans for escape were made and a hidden radio was operated... but the Japanese discovered the radio and arrested those involved. They were then executed.

Though Stanley was rife with rumours, the first real indication that the war was over came when American planes dropped leaflets urging prisoners to remain in camp to await relief.

On August 30, 1945, came the Hong Kong Government's first communique since the Union Jack had been lowered on that bleak Christmas Day of 1941: "Rear Admiral Harcourt is lying outside Hong Kong with a very strong fleet..."

In the new tiered and turreted Government House on September 16, 1945, Vice Admiral Ruitako Fujita and Major General Umekichi Okada, watched by military observers from America, China and Canada stood behind a small table bearing brushes and an ink slab. Admiral Harcourt read the Surrender Document.

When the document had been acknowledged by signatures and inked characters, the Japanese handed over their swords, bowed stiffly from the waist and were marched away.

Outside Government House the Royal Marine Band struck up the national anthem and, as it was being played, an able seaman very slowly hoisted the Union Jack.

Then the harbour below thundered the triumphant salute of every warship, and the Fleet Air Arm roared approval overhead.

Everywhere was rubble, desolation and hunger.

The harbour was jammed with wrecks that would cost more than a million dollars to clear. The godowns were empty, the docks reduced to ruins. Factories, offices and homes had been ransacked or destroyed. The fishing fleet was decimated.

The population had been reduced by one million, and most people had no money, no homes, no food or fuel.

Ex-PoWs laughed ironically at the fact that they had harbour-view rooms at one of the world's most exclusive hotels — with no food, water, lights or lifts!

But as always at "The Pen" there was plenty of talk: talk of the end of foreign concessions in China; talk of the end of extra territoriality; talk of the end of empire.

Though Churchill had doggedly refused to return Hong

Kong to Chiang Kai Shek at the Cairo Conference, there was still talk of the end of Hong Kong.

As rumours multiplied the emaciated, war-weary population went quickly back to work in make shift offices, using borrowed equipment, making urgent plans over tables covered with blankets.

Civil servants, businessmen, bankers and clerks came out of Stanley to a battle of a different kind: re-establishing the British administration of Hong Kong.

The Navy hauled away the wrecks. Warships were dispatched to buy food and fuel. Repair work began on wharves, buildings, ships and homes — and went on day and night.

Everyone understood instinctively that survival lay in shedding the grim mantle of a war-torn city with phenomenal speed.

Soon warehouses were restocked; ferries, trams and trains were running; shops and offices reopened, and factories began taking on workers from the limitless pool of refugee labour crossing the border.

"The Pen" ripped down its Japanese name and began welcoming tycoons and world travellers.

The Governor replaced shoji screens, Formosan pine with the familiarity of flowered cretonnes, crystal and silver.

Government House began dispatching those coveted gilt-edged cards, inviting the world to view the city port that had risen from the ashes of war.

And the Noonday Gun, symbol of the free port since its opium-running days, began to boom out across the harbour once again.

Hong Kong had always appreciated the necessity of making a show, of striding out of a tough spot with what seemed like the old bold effrontery of empire, but might just have been a gambler's good joss.

Certainly it acknowledged the end of an era, the loss of some assets. But already it was juggling a new set of assets: it had now become the only place on the China coast where the British could live and trade under their own laws; and every day it was inheriting from war torn China the labour, capital and technical skills that could fuel an industrial revolution.

Clearly Hong Kong was on the threshold of a new era and new ventures — a situation that called for consultation on a spiritual level...

The *feng shui* man would reassure Hong Kong of its favourable location, pointing to the essential harmony of wind and water and the proximity of dragon spirits in the mountains of China.

The fortune teller would advise that though things had changed, they remained the same. For a new Son of Heaven was gathering strength to rule the Celestial Empire from Peking, and foreigners would again be banished to the empire's outer limits.

Hong Kong would continue to offer — as in the beginning — a place for foreign traders on the doorstep of China.

And thus would continue to serve both the Lion and the Dragon.

The "barren island" Lord Palmerston so derided was known to Chinese fishermen who chased shoals across the South China Sea, and to the clipper ships that favoured its safe harbour. In the wake of the merchants came the forces that would defend Britain's "ancient rights of commerce". Well before the signing of the Treaty of Peking in 1862 Anglo-French North China expeditionary forces, accommodated in tents, had occupied sections of the Kowloon peninsula (previous page).

Military parades — like this one in May of 1862 — became a familiar spectacle as Britain's empire spread to cover a quarter of the world. In Hong Kong the troops based in the colony, or passing through on an expeditionary force bound for China, bolstered the security of the island on the doorstep of China.

In 1869 Queen Victoria's younger son, the Duke of Edinburgh became Hong Kong's first royal visitor.
He opened Hong Kong's fine new City Hall and laid the foundation stone for the chancel of
St John's Cathedral. Long boats drawn up in review marked the Duke's route when he arrived
on the frigate HMS *Galatea*.

Hong Kong's clock tower — symbol of civic pride in the Victorian era — chimed the hour for the
first time on New Year's Eve in 1862. It is seen (opposite) under construction from Queen's Road looking
west, and (above) from Pedder Street. It was later demolished as a traffic hazard. Its clock was provided
by taipan Douglas Lapraik, who began his Hong Kong career as a watchmaker's assistant.

Douglas Lapraik (left) arrived in Hong Kong in the 1840's and thirteen years later owned docks,
had founded a shipping company and built himself a miniature castle.
(Above) Hong Kong's Executive Council in 1860: the Governor, Sir Hercules Robinson,
wearing a top hat, with (left to right) the Colonial Secretary Mr William Mercer, Mr Leslie,
and Colonel Haythorne, the Captain Superintendent of Police.
The Council comprised only three members for its first 30 years.

The staff of Dent & Co in 1861: one of a number of prominent local firms whose demise was brought about by the failure of a major London Bank.

An informal picture of the staff of the Hongkong and Shanghai Bank taken at St. John's Place in February 1886.
The bank first opened for business in 1865 at a time when all transactions were conducted in silver.
Its bullion boat was soon a familiar sight in the harbour. It was called *Wayfoong*, meaning
"Abundance of Remittances" — the bank's Chinese name.

Top hats and extravagantly pretty bonnets crowded the grandstand at Happy Valley race course in 1861 when weekly races were held. The beautiful track lay in a valley that had been drained to rid it of mosquitoes, and levelled to facilitate the itch for punting that equally afflicted Chinese and British residents.

Prior to the appearance of rickshaws, sedan chairs were the most favoured mode of transport. Chinese ladies of
status seldom ventured out, except behind the shutters or silken curtains of a ladies' chair (opposite).
There were two-man chairs for hire at public places, four-man chairs with bearers in livery for the wealthy,
and eight-man chairs for the colony's top brass. The Governor's scarlet-curtained sedan was instantly recognizable in Hong Kong.

33

Previous page: View of Hong Kong harbour in 1910. Above: The original Government House, boasted a 60 ft ballroom,
billiard and supper rooms and a large staff of pigtailed servants in long blue satin gowns.
Above and opposite: Views before and after the new chancel was added to St John's Cathedral in 1872 rendering
the somewhat small ''cathedral'' more worthy of the name.

Classical colonial buildings lined the praya, then rose tier upon tier up the lower flanks of the Peak.
Following reclamation on the waterfront, the praya became Des Voeux Road.

After Hong Kong was flattened by a typhoon in its first year of existence, it became used to
the task of rebuilding itself. But the typhoon of September 22, 1874 was described as the worst
in living memory. Damage was extensive and more than two thousand lost their lives in six terrible hours.

"The rain descended in torrents. The wind blew with the violence of a tempest, the rage of a whirlwind. Vessels staunch and strong were driven hither and thither like children's toy craft..." *The Hong Kong Telegraph*'s graphic description of the typhoon of 1874 which beached paddle boats and wrecked sailing ships.

In 1898 Hong Kong embraced a new slice of Chinese territory — the New Territories. With its walled clan villages, rice paddies, ancestral halls and secluded bays, it was an area that retained the unhurried pace of its farmers and fisherfolk. Cantonese farmers worked the most arable land, leaving what remained for the hardy Hakkas.

The fertile Shatin Valley produced two fine crops of rice a year. The first was used by villagers,
the second was sent as a tribute to the Emperor in Peking. People in the valley liked to call it "the Emperor's rice bowl",
and all enjoyed its harvest. Opposite: Cultivation and weaving of silk, an ancient industry, was established on
Sir Robert Ho Tung's New Territories farm, far from the silk centres of China.

45

Opposite: The New Territories lease stipulated that Kowloon Walled City should remain under Chinese
control. When the British revoked the clause, Chinese opinion refused to acknowledge this and
control of the six-acre walled city remained in dispute. It became a refuge for criminals,
and a haven for secret societies and gamblers.

Imperial China devised an array of punishments ranging from flogging, face-slapping and the
humiliation of the wooden cangue, previous page, left. There were also several varieties of capital punishment.
The pirates opposite were beheaded in Kowloon City in 1891. Grave robbers were left to die,
heads protruding from crates — possibly a similar fate as shown above.

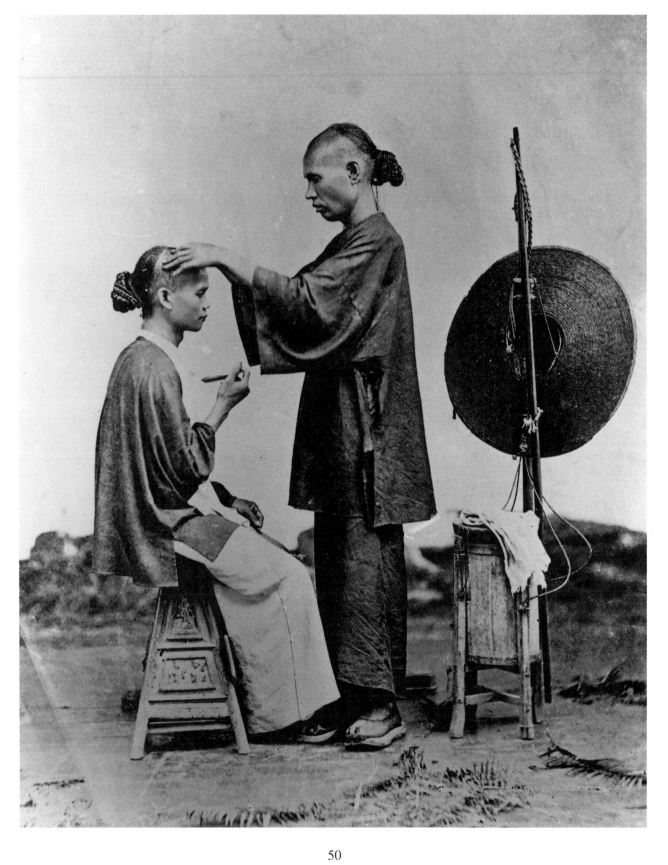

A cobbler working on the distinctive white-soled shoes favoured by Chinese in the
19th century. Like most hawkers, he set up shop wherever demand existed, and carried the
tools of his trade in baskets suspended from a shoulder pole. Opposite: A streetside hairdresser.

Opposite: Merchant and his son in 1861. Above: Chinese merchants, whose status in
the hierarchy of Chinese society changed radically as the colony and China opened to foreign trade.

In Hong Kong the Chinese menu had an exotic range, from civet cat to snake — both favoured to
keep out the cold of winter. These merchants around a blackwood dinner table, set with porcelain bowls and ivory chopsticks,
might boast swallows' nest soup or golden Peking duck, served with fiery rice wine.

Street markets were colourful features in the Hong Kong of the 1880s. Huge cane baskets were filled with
fresh produce from the colony's market gardens and the mainland. Above: A young
businessman elegantly dressed for Chinese New Year festivities.

The plague, erupting in Victoria's worst slums in 1894, claimed thousands of lives. Resentment mounted as the sick and dying were removed from fever-stricken areas to temporary plague hospitals (opposite). Thousands fled back to China, and the coffins of many victims were shipped by junk back to the mainland (above).

Elaborate rituals and prolonged mourning surrounded death. Bamboo staircases, constructed
as exit routes for the coffin, helped to foil malevolent spirits. The wealthy were farewelled
in extravagant style; the poor had paper luxuries burnt at funerals to ensure them
greater comfort in the afterlife.

Previous pages: Hong Kong became an important centre for Chinese emigration, as free emigrants and
contract coolie labour embarked for foreign shores. Above: The crippling custom of foot
binding originated to prevent women straying, then persisted for erotic and aesthetic reasons.
Men found the ''golden lily'' foot measuring no more than five inches both attractive and titillating.

Li Hung Chang, who was in charge of the Board of Foreign Affairs in China until 1898 when he was dismissed
for having obliged the Dowager Empress with naval funds to rebuild the Summer Palace. He travelled abroad on missions
and was well liked by Europeans for his tact and charm. He refused to comply with an imperial edict
to join the Boxer Rebellion's attacks on foreigners and Chinese Christians. He is photographed above seated next to Sir Henry Blake
at Government House in 1900, while on a diplomatic visit relating to negotiations on the Kowloon Walled City.

At the height of empire in 1898, British vessels were never far from a British port
with docks, coaling stations and naval bases. Above: A group of officers on
coaling duty in 1898. Opposite: HMS *Powerful* coaling, with HMS *Tamar*
in the background.

Previous page: By the turn of the century Hong Kong had become the second largest port in Asia and
its busy harbour offered a breathtaking view from the Peak. Above: From the highest
summit to the bluest bay, there was ample scope for recreation —
as Margery Holland's 1898 boat picnic at Deep Water Bay illustrates.

Polo and cricket were probably the most popular recreations for civilians and members of the forces in the far-flung outposts of empire. It was an easy stroll to the Cricket Club in Central, but bicycles and rickshaws were preferable when going to the East Point polo ground in 1899.

The Chinese Recreation Club beach outing in 1917 and (opposite) the staff of Lane Crawford in 1904.

Lane Crawford conducted auctions, supplied water to ships in harbour, and opened a waterfront store
where one could reputedly buy anything from a pin to an anchor. Enterprise paid off and T.A. Lane,
once a government clerk, and Ninian Crawford, a humble store clerk, ended up owning the colony's most fashionable
department store, with branches in Shanghai, Yokohama and Kobe. Above: Relaxing in Lane Crawford's mess, 1904.
Opposite: The store's tailoring department.

Sir Henry May was Colonial Secretary before becoming Governor of Hong Kong. An enthusiastic sportsman, he enjoyed riding, fishing, game-shooting and golf — all of which he encouraged. This photograph of Sir Henry in full riding gear with whip was taken in 1908. Opposite: A decade later the great fire at Happy Valley at Chinese New Year claimed six hundred lives when spectators were trapped in the fiercely-burning matshed stands.

There was little warning from the Hong Kong Observatory when the gun boomed across the
harbour in 1906 heralding a devastating typhoon. More than eleven thousand lost their lives and
forty-one merchant ships were driven ashore. Warnings of approaching typhoons came from
the Jesuit fathers who ran the Manila weather bureau.

Opposite: South African medals were presented to members of the Sherwood Foresters, a Derbyshire
Regiment, when the First Battalion came to Hong Kong in 1903/4. Above: The arrival of
Sir Frederick Lugard, who became Governor in 1907. With a distinguished military career in Africa behind him,
Lugard would go on to become one of the elder statesmen of empire.

The wedding in 1906 of Lieutenant Commander C.W. Beckworth, assistant harbour master, which was attended by Sir Frederick Lugard. Opposite: The Governor with the Viceroy of Canton on the steps of Government House. Viceroy Chang Jen Chuh requested a tour of the Taikoo Docks during his visit, having plans to dredge the Pearl River to develop a deepwater port at Whampoa.

The opening of the Peak Tram in 1888 make residence on the Peak more practical —
provided you could secure the permit to reside on its hallowed heights. The tram
completed the journey in fifteen minutes and the front seat was reserved for the
Governor who, with the rest of Hong Kong's high society, enjoyed Peak summer retreats.

Queen's College, which began its life in the 1870s as the Central School and was later renamed Victoria College, boasted a handsome building in Aberdeen Street. Initially a mixed school for boys of all nationalities, it accepted only Chinese pupils from 1903.

On his arrival in 1907 Sir Frederick Lugard advocated the foundation of a university in Hong Kong, and immediately money was offered for the main building by Sir Hormusjee Mody. A subscription list was opened and many other companies and individuals donated. The government provided a site at West Point and the foundation stone was laid by Lugard in 1910. Opposite: Sir Frederick Lugard opening St Paul's School in 1911.

Opium, originally eaten raw as a medicine, was mixed with tobacco and smoked from the
17th century in China. Though its cultivation and import were banned, addiction spread in
China — even the Emperor's eunuchs and bodyguards were addicted. In 1909 an International
Opium Conference in Shanghai (above) consolidated opposition to the trade. Two years earlier the
Hong Kong Government had closed all local divans.

Royal Square, reclaimed from the harbour, became the perfect site for monuments to the majesty of empire.
It would eventually accommodate several royal statues, including one of Queen Alexandra,
unveiled by the Governor, Sir Frederick Lugard, on November 25, 1909 — the birthday of King Edward VII.

Plumed helmets, pith helmets and straw boaters were much in evidence when Hong Kong
gave one of the British Empire's most famous figures a suitably dignified formal welcome.
Lord Kitchener visited Hong Kong in 1909 at a time when the empire spanned a quarter of the world.
It was the largest empire in history, and Hong Kong was just one of a galaxy of imperial islands.

Opposite: The grandmother of Sir Man Kam Lo, founder of the firm Lo and Lo and next to her,
Sir Robert Ho Tung's wife, Margaret. Above: Louisa Landale, wife of the Jardine, Matheson taipan in 1919
and Yeu Yung Ling, a former lady-in-waiting to the Dowager Empress, photographed
in Hong Kong in 1910.

The family of Jardine's comprador, Robert Ho Tung, were prominent in Hong Kong.
Robert Ho Tung joined the "noble house" of Jardine, Matheson as a shipping clerk, and
amassed considerable power and wealth. Opposite: Sisters Florence and Flora Ho at the Aberdeen
waterfall in 1911. Above: Members of the Ho Fook and Ho Kam Tong family,
who had just returned from studies in England in 1904.

Parsee merchants established wholesale businesses in Hong Kong and formed a community of considerable influence.
The Parsees were followed by Hindus and Moslems. Jangir Ruttonjee and his wife Banoo (opposite)
arrived from India in 1892. Jangir became an important member of the Indian community,
his family name surviving in the Ruttonjee Sanitorium and the recently completed Ruttonjee Centre.

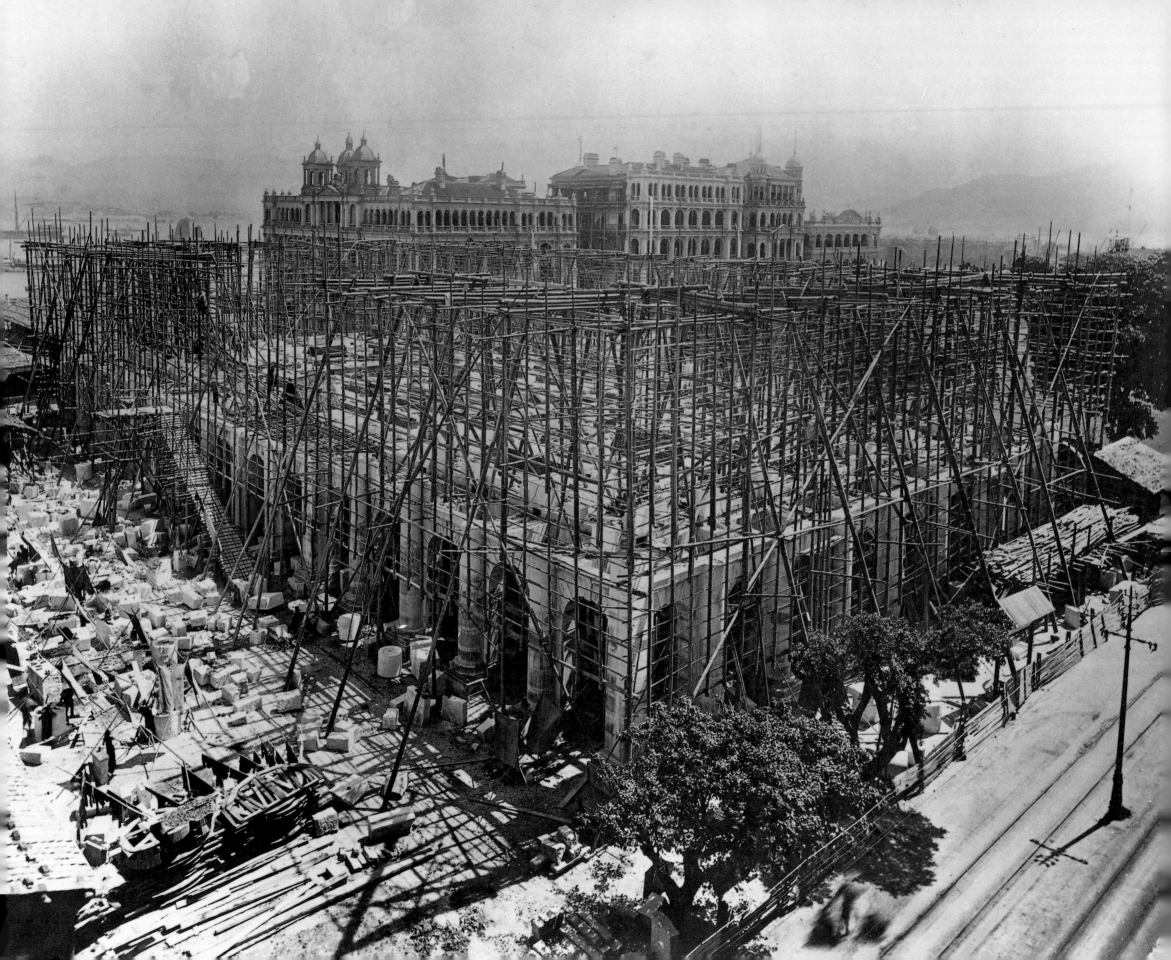

Within years of the colony's establishment it had a Supreme Court, and in 1903 work
began on the fine domed court building (designed by Aston Webb) which would eventually
accommodate the court staff. Above: Offices of Butterfield and Swire, the Great Northern
Telegraph Company and the Hong Kong Club in 1906.

The festive atmosphere of the coronation celebrations was enhanced with decorated trams and
dragon dances. In Queen's Road Central the 100-man dragon dance performance was drastically reduced from
the usual three or four hours to fit in with the busy programme of official events
and to avoid undue congestion.

On October 10, 1910 Henry May as Colonial Secretary and a trainload of dignitaries were the first passengers
to travel on the British section of the Kowloon-Canton Railway. A year later the Chinese
section of the track had been completed. Opposite: Governor Lugard with top hat attending the official opening.
In the centre is Li Cheng Feng, Commissioner of Foreign Affairs, and seated beside him Cecil Clementi.

Sedan chairs — along with pith helmets and punkahs — were symbols of empire. But in 1912 when
Sir Frederick Lugard left Hong Kong (above) the days of the sedan were nearly over. The pace of life was quickening,
an era of unhurried elegance was ending, and the sedan was headed for the scrap-heap. Lugard's successor May
would own one of the colony's first cars, setting a trend that would result in many sedans being abandoned. Opposite:
Discarded chairs became a common sight — affording moments of amusement to those they had once carried.

Sir Henry May, formerly Colonial Secretary, became Governor of Hong Kong in 1912 at a time when the mainland was convulsed in revolution and Europe was on the brink of a devastating war. He was photographed in 1910 with officers of the Hong Kong Regiment, which was stationed in the colony from the 1880s.

Governor May's term of office was marked by the completion of many important public works,
including the rebuilding of the Central Police Station. In 1915, when this photograph was taken,
the Governor visited the station for a presentation ceremony and inspection parade.

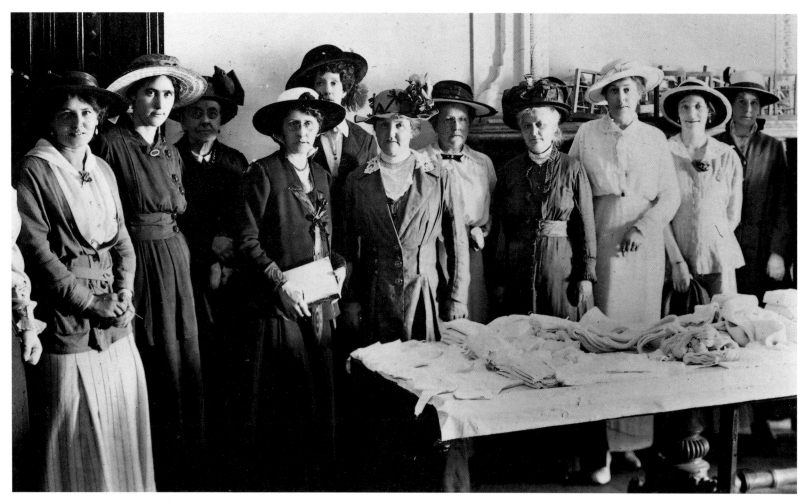

During World War I, Hong Kong provided a safe harbour far from the horrors of warfare.
Previous pages: Inspection of a parade of two hundred and forty members of the Hong Kong volunteer Corps, and sixty-one reserves accompanied by the band of the 8th Rajput Regiment on Murray parade ground in 1913. Above: A work party packing bandages at the City Hall, and (right) machine gun instructions on the balcony of the Peninsula Hotel before its completion.

HMS *Terrible* staged a patriotic salute — its letters formed entirely by sailors suspended
from the side of the ship — to mark peace. Hong Kong had shared the anguish of its allies in the
darkest hours of the long war, and when the armistice came the city centre
blossomed with Allied flags.

When the Prince of Wales was asked how he would like to be entertained on his visit
in 1922, he expressed a loathing for overlong banquets and a love of polo.
Governor Sir Reginald Stubbs and his wife organised a four-course banquet and a game of polo
Above: The Prince taking the royal salute at Blake Pier. Opposite: At Government House the Prince of Wales
flanked by Governor and Miss Stubbs, with Louis Mountbatten behind the Prince.

Aerial view of Hong Kong when the waterfront ran along Connaught Road. Opposite: The magnificent City Hall, built largely from funds donated by Jardine, Matheson, and the water fountain that graced its forecourt, donated by Jardine's rival John Dent. The City Hall complex was opened by the Duke of Edinburgh in 1869.

The Hongkong and Shanghai Bank, which opened in 1865, occupied in 1883 a fine Victorian building with a circular banking hall under a copper dome. It looked on to Royal Square, and a statue of its former chief manager, Sir Thomas "Lucky" Jackson.

Opposite: In 1887 the Duke of Connaught laid the foundation stone for the reclamation which
would provide the site for this bronze statue of King Edward VII. Seventeen years later he unveiled the statue.
Above: Looking north to Royal Square, and the bronze statue of Queen Victoria.

(Previous pages) The unveiling ceremony of the new Cenotaph on May 24, 1923.
(Above) The Kowloon-Canton Railway terminus heralded a romantic era of rail travel
when it opened in 1910. Soon travellers would be able to board a luxury train in Hong Kong, travel across the vast
landscapes of China and Russia, and disembark in Paris.

Aerial view of the Peninsula Hotel in 1930, two years after the hotel opened. "The Pen" with its ritzy marble lobby became a favourite rendezvous for tycoons and travellers. When the Japanese occupied Hong Kong they renamed it the Toa Hotel, and initially it served as their headquarters.

Since the early days, when waterfront opportunists began their own private reclamation (which was eventually forbidden) Hong Kong began reclaiming land from the seabed. Above: Causeway Bay before reclamation. Opposite: Markers indicate the proposed shoreline for the Wanchai reclamation.

Members of the Catholic Choa Po Sien family (opposite) whose home in Hong Kong became
a meeting place for Jesuit missionaries travelling in China during the 1920s. In earlier
centuries the Jesuits had held privileged positions in Peking due to their knowledge
of mathematics and astronomy.

137

In 1920 George Bernard Shaw and his wife Margaret were entertained by Hong Kong's most famous comprador, Sir Robert Ho Tung. Also photographed are Ho Tung's son, Ho Shai Lai and R.K. Simpson, Professor of English Literature at Hong Kong University, and Mrs Simpson.

Dr Sun Yat Sen (centre front row) at Hong Kong University. Dr Sun studied at the Hong Kong College of
Medicine, but when his anti-Manchu activities made him conspicuous, he was asked to leave
the colony on the grounds that Hong Kong could not be made a base for subversive activities against
China. When the Chinese Republic was proclaimed in 1911, Dr Sun became its first President.

Number One House was erected on the East Point site purchased by Jardines at the first land auction
held in 1841. In 1923 Lee Hysan made an offer Jardines could not refuse and they finally yielded
the elegant site with an emotional farewell party.
Number One was the scene of the wedding of Lee Hysan's daughter in the mid-1930s.

Fire devastated the infant city in the 1840s and continued to plague the colony's congested centre.
Police stood by to guard against looting as this fire which raged
in the Hong Kong Hotel, one of the Colony's leading luxury hotels,
was fought by soldiers of the East Surrey Regiment.

A view of Pedder Street from the old General Post
Office, with the Hong Kong Hotel on the left. Opposite: The Post Office, with its
distinctive alternating red Amoy brickwork, which was built in 1903 on the corner of
Pedder Street and Des Voeux Road.

On the eve of the Japanese attack, orders were issued to sink any potentially useful vessels. HMS *Tamar* was scuttled four days after the Japanese crossed the border. At first she resolutely refused to sink — the superstructure providing administrative accommodation above her decks became airlocked — and the Royal Artillery had to hasten her demise. However, her name lived on.

Before it became a colony, Hong Kong was a refuge for pirates who plundered the trading ships that
sailed along the China coast. Piracy continued to threaten shipping well into the 20th century.
These manacled pirates and their captors were photographed on HMS *Ostend* in 1927.

Hong Kong's most famous hongs and institutional banks set a trend for bachelor living back
in the old days of empire. Though the social situation changed, the colony offered
numerous all-male retreats — like the club or the mess — where a man could enjoy a curry tiffin
and escape the midday sun.

Crossing the harbour in 1930 on the *Northern Star*, this would have been your first impression of Hong Kong island's bustling waterfront. The elegant facades of the Hong Kong Club and Queen's Building were typical of the architecture of empire.

Church schools, run by the Anglican and Catholic churches, were the first to open in the early years.
In 1847 the government gave its first grants to three traditional Chinese schools for boys,
but it was not until 1890 that a government school for girls was opened. Above: Traditional once a year
formal staff portrait with the local patron and financial supporters of St Stephen's Girls School.
Opposite: Headmistress Miss Middleton-Smith and Miss Atkins in the staff sitting room in 1925.

Sir Paul and Lady Chater (centre) with Frank Nipper Deacon (left), John Theophilus Bagram and Mrs Deacon in front of the Repulse Bay Hotel in 1921. Descended from Armenian princes, Chater had an unerring instinct for making a fortune — from real estate or a punt at Happy Valley. He lived in a mansion called "Marble Hall", kept race horses and served on the Legislative Council.

The Colonial Secretary, Sir Thomas Southorn, and Lady Southorn photographed in 1936. Back row from left, Tang Siu Kin, John Henry Burkhill Lee, cadet officer, to become Postmaster General after the war, L.G. Bird of Palmer and Turner, architects, and in uniform (front row) D.R. Black, Volunteer Decoration Lieut. Colonel Field Ambulance and H.W.L. Dowbiggin, commanding officer of the Hong Kong Volunteer Defence Corps.

Aeroplanes first touched down, sometimes upside down, at Kai Tak in 1924 on a square of grass just big
enough for the era's small machines. The airport was named after two Chinese
businessmen, Kai Ho Ai and Au Tak. The government took over the airport in
1927 three years before this fire in one of the matshed hangars.

In the old days a Chinese bride would be carried to her wedding in an ornamental
sedan chair, but this bride photographed in 1936 was probably driven to her ceremony in a car.
The bride was Miss Chan, who wore the traditional wedding gown of her native Shanghai.
The groom was Mr Yam Man Lo.

It was very much a Royal Navy wedding when Pamela Poland, daughter of Captain Allan
Poland, the Commanding Officer of HMS *Medway*, married Commander C.T. Addis of that ship
at St John's Cathedral in 1933.

Immediately following the collapse of the Ching Dynasty which had dominated China for 268 years
Western hats replaced shaven heads and pigtails which Chinese men had worn as symbols
of Manchu domination.

The bright blooms of Wyndham Street could not dispel Hong Kong's anxiety on the eve of war. Many of the
colony's Japanese barbers and dentists had been busy gathering information which would prove invaluable to
the invaders in 1941. The view of the Hongkong and Shanghai Bank, opposite, was taken by employee
Frank Smark and kept throughout internment in Sham Sui Po; the harbour scene, symbolic of the conflict to come,
was taken by leading seaman J.F. Gregory of HMS Submarine *Rainbow*, who lost his life during the war.
He was a member of the Royal Photographic Society.

Though it had been assured it was an "impregnable fortress", Hong Kong was ill equipped
to wage war against the battle-hardened Japanese army in 1941. Japanese planes bombed
the airport, harbour and dockyard repair shops extensively before assaulting the island,
which surrendered on Christmas Day, 1941.

Exploiting the internal troubles of China, Japan began seizing territory and was at war with China by 1937.
Lieutenant General Sakai crossed the land border in Fanling on December 18, 1941 with two divisions,
reserving his crack third division in readiness for the island's invasion. As the Japanese Army swept through China,
many civilian Chinese fled to Hong Kong. After the colony surrendered, Singapore fell and Japan was master
of the Far Eastern seas. These group portraits were taken at Whampoa Dockyards in 1942.

After the fall of Hong Kong, Japanese authorities ordered the liquidation of the Hongkong and Shanghai Bank and demanded the assistance of the bank's staff. The process took until mid-1943, during which time bank staff were accommodated in a Chinese hotel, and were marched to and from their former offices each day.

Japanese occupation brought the colony to a standstill and reduced its population by one million. Unable to feed the people, the occupying army forced them to return to China. Above: The annual celebration of the Japanese Emperor's birthday on April 29 at the Whampoa Docks during the years of occupation.

When Japan surrendered in September 1945 POWs who had been interned for four years
were released from Stanley Internment Camp to fight another battle — re-establishing
British administration in the devastated colony.

Opposite: Japanese officials, with brush and ink, put their signatures to the Surrender Document
while in contrast the British signatures were penned with a brisk flourish at the stark ceremony in Government House
on September 16, 1945. Military observers from several Allied nations watched as Major General Umekichi Okada
signed the document with Mr Makimura, Commissioner for Foreign Affairs, at his side.
Captain J.A.S. Eccles is standing, hands clasped, and at centre the officer wearing aiguillettes is
Rear Admiral Harcourt's secretary.

Photographic sources

Appreciation is extended to the following institutions and individuals who made their collections available for the preparation of this book.

Lieutenant Commander C.P. Addis MBE
Gloria Barretto
Peggy Beard collection
Derek Bird
Patricia Body
British Broadcasting Corporation Hulton Library
The British Library
Andrew Choa
The Commonwealth Institute
Leo Cooper
Vera Desai
Essex Institute, Massachusetts
Foreign and Commonwealth Office Research Department
Foreign Office Library
Michael Forrer
George Eastman House
Peter Hall
Robert Ho
Honeychurch Antiques, Hong Kong
Hongkong and Shanghai Banking Corporation
Hong Kong and Whampoa Dock Co.
Robin Hutcheon
Images of the past — Stockhouse
Imperial War Museum
India Office Library
Sir Michael Jackson
Kodak International Museum of Photography
John Swire and Sons Ltd

Kyodo News Agency, Tokyo
Lam Chik Seun
Lane Crawford Ltd
Rev. Lee Chi Kong
Leung Sai Wa
Matheson and Co. Ltd
Brian McElney
Rear Admiral M.A. McMullen CE OBE
National Maritime Museum
National Register of Archives, Scotland
Photography in Imperial China by Clark Worswick
Pitt Rivers Museum
Public Records Office of Hong Kong
Lady Ride
Rhodes House Library, Oxford
Royal Artillary Institution, Woolwich
Royal Asiatic Society, London
Royal Engineers, Medway
Royal Engineers Corps Library, Chatham
Royal Geographical Society, London
Royal Naval Museum
Royal Navy Volunteers
Peter Schlipf, Landau's, Hong Kong
School of Oriental and African Studies
South China Morning Post
St. Stephen's Girls College
The Captain in Charge H.M.S. Tamar
Andrew Tse
University of Hong Kong Library — Hong Kong collection
University of Nottingham Library
Thomas G. Vine
Welcome Institute for the History of Medicine

Acknowledgements

It is obvious that the concept of stray photographs collectively telling the story of old Hong Kong could only become a reality as a result of the enthusiastic involvement of friends who provided a rich fund of contacts as sources of photographs of old Hong Kong. To the following friends we offer our special thanks:

Ken Barnett OBE
Colonel H.A. de Botelho
Ronald Boxall
Charles and Rosamund Brown
George and Ruby Cautherley
Benno Gross
Charlotte Havilland
Erica and George Hinden
Keith and Elsie Kerr
Kwong Chung Kwan
Margaret Lee
David K.P. Li
David Mahoney

Neil Maidment
Robyn McLean
Stuart Muirhead
Ranjit Peiris
Ginty and Stuart Read
Elizabeth Sinn
Angela and Terzani Tiziano
Glenn and Lucille Vessa
Zenobia Wetzell
Anita Wilson
Yoichi Yakobori
Peter Yeung